Black Forest Dreams

A Journey Through Germany

Black Forest Dreams

A Journey Through Germany

Poems by

Joseph Kuhn Carey

Cover design by Shay Culligan
Cover photograph of a beautiful Seitingen-Oberflacht sunset
by Alexander Doderer

Library of Congress Control Number: 2021903023
ISBN: 978-1-952326-75-2

Kelsay Books
502 South 1040 East, A-119
American Fork, Utah, 84003

For Renata, Joey and Nicholas,
my three northern stars,
guiding me through life, love,
hope, travel and song,

and for Mom and Dad,
my shining beautiful beacons
in both day and night

Acknowledgments

To my wife, Renata, and sons, Joey and Nicholas, for all the joy they've brought me as we've traveled on vacations as a family across the United States, Europe and Africa, enjoying the experiences of so many different and beautiful cultures. Thanks, too, for listening to my poems so many times over the dinner table after meals; your commentary, feedback, support and love was much appreciated!

To my Mom and Dad, Bill and Helen Carey, who instilled a love of adventure & travel in me at a young age by telling so many great stories about Dad's travels over oceans and seas to numerous colorful foreign ports of call as a Lieutenant in the U.S. Navy during the Korean War (and who continued to travel around the world and enthrall their three children with their experiences in other far-flung countries!). Thanks, too, Mom & Dad, for all of the wonderful books you gave us each Christmas Eve, which inspired us to enjoy the glorious interplay of words, thoughts and ideas and get wonderfully lost for hours in a bed, chair, corner or couch with a riveting read.

To my grandparents, Joseph and Theresia Kuhn, and my great uncle, Reinhold Lehmann, all born in the Black Forest and brave enough to leave their pastoral, wooded home to journey to America and pursue their hopes, passions and dreams.

For Janet Burroway, my wonderful mentor, spiritual writing guide, supporter and friend for many years.

To the amazing, mystical and magical Steve Katz, my first creative writing teacher in college, whose recommendation letter helped to somehow shoehorn me into the University of Iowa Writers' Workshop and who continued to encourage me over the years with postcards, letters, e-mails and occasional calls. Thanks for all of the superb support, Steve! May you always sail on soft soothing heaven-sent winds in cloudless clear blue Colorado skies.

For James Marran, the finest high school history teacher a teenaged kid could ever encounter. Thanks for inspiring me to fall in love with digging into the past in search of hidden historical treasures.

For Jennifer Dotson, the founder of Highland Park Poetry, who published my first poems and continues to guide my poetry path with kindness, insight, gentleness and joy.

Lastly, to all those who accept the fine-spun golden gift of travel, who venture away from home to see the world!

"Black Forest Dreams" Poetry Collection Awards (under the previous manuscript name "Back To The Black Forest"):

—2017 Paris Book Festival, Winner, "Travel" Category (May 2017)

—2016 Amsterdam Book Festival, Winner, "Travel" Category (May 2016)

—2016 Northern California Book Festival, Winner, "Travel" Category (October 2016)

—2017 Los Angeles Book Festival, Honorable Mention, "Poetry" Category (March 2017)

—2017 Great Southeast Book Festival, Honorable Mention, "Poetry" Category (March 2017)

—2016 London Book Festival, Honorable Mention, "Poetry" Category (December 2016)

—2016 New York Book Festival, Honorable Mention, "Poetry" Category (June 2016)

Individual "Black Forest Dreams" Poem Awards and Individual Poem Publication Locations:

"Night Knows" was selected as a first-place award winner in the 2016 Highland Park Poetry Challenge Contest. "Deer Bridges" was selected in the "Poets and Patrons" 62nd annual poetry contest in 2016. "Red and Green Men" was selected in the "Poets & Patrons" 61st annual poetry contest in 2015. "Watching the Scenery" appeared in the Highland Park Poetry website's Muses' Gallery of poems in January 2017. "The Lady From Dubai" appeared on the Illinois State Poetry Society's website in August 2015. "Thinking of Germany" was selected in the Illinois State Poetry Society's 2015 Poetry Contest and appeared in the ISPS Newsletter in January 2015. A version of "Floating in a Pool" appeared in "East on Central" in 2015. "Two Man Crosscut Saw" and "In the Open Cable Car" appeared in the Journal of Modern Poetry's JOMP 18 Poetry Collection in 2015. "In the Open Cable Car" also appeared in the Highland Park Poetry website's Muses' Gallery in 2013. "Grandma Kuhn's Plumcake" appeared in the Highland Park Poetry's website's Muses' Gallery in 2014. "A Silent Prayer" appeared in the Highland Park Poetry website's Muses' Gallery in 2013. "The Thermal Pool" appeared in the Fall 2019 Muses' Gallery on the Highland Park Poetry website. "The Munich McDonald's" appeared on the Illinois State Poetry Society's website in 2020. "Ice Cream on a Bench" appeared in an Illinois State Poetry Society travel poetry display in Chicagoland public libraries in 2017. "Carriage Ride of Dreams" appeared in the Illinois State Poetry Society's *Distilled Lives, Volume 5* poetry collection in 2020.

Contents

The Black Forest Is a Dream

The Black Forest
is a dream,
a mysterious
mingling of woods, paths,
roads and streams, where
past and present join hands
and deftly dance across
the alluring landscape
until all you hear is a
sweet simple folk song
and all you see is a scythe,
a spoon, a motorcycle,
a boy and a girl and
love & hope flickering
in an old black and white movie
on a stucco farmhouse wall
surrounded by the deep dark quietude
of the beautiful green countryside,
rolling, endless, expanding, serene.

Grandma's Wooden Spoon

Grandma's wooden spoon
sits proudly in the drawer,
smooth as silk from years of use,
easy to handle, full of love,
ready to turn again in circles
like the hand of time itself
to make her reappear, bustling
here and there in a colorful apron,
making culinary magic with the
wave of her wondrous wand,
the kitchen full of glorious smells,
the pots bubbling, each with
mysterious good things to eat,
the clean old white-topped table
ready with silverware and plates,
before a few last-minute samples and sips
at the stove to make sure everything is
just as it should be before the
hearty two-meat, three vegetable
lunchtime feast is set down before
many happy hungry sets of eyes.

Thinking of Germany

Thinking of Germany,
of Black Forest relatives unseen
for forty years,
of the house (still there)
that Grandma Kuhn and her
brother (my godfather) Reinhold grew up in,
way down south in tiny Seitingen-Oberflacht,
where farming was a way of life,
and steady muscles were required
for milking the cows and feeding the chickens,
unloading train cars full of wood and
using a heavy scythe to cut the tall fields of
grass, or working in the ziegelhütte,
the clay tile-making barn in the winter,
digging deep for the clay and putting it in molds
for kilning into solid forms for roofing use,
hard, hard work for little return while all of
the other brothers and sisters left for America
and the depression between the wars hit,
requiring a wheelbarrow full of worthless paper money
to buy a loaf of bread, until there was nothing to do but start over
in a country new in every way, where they didn't know the
language or the customs, but had relatives waiting with open arms,
and jobs no one wanted to do for them to grab,
packing up and leaving it all behind, everything they knew
for the complete unknown, while other relatives stayed
behind to take over the house and farm and keep the distant
home fires burning, waiting for a return at some future
as yet undetermined time,
the scythe hangs heavy on the shed wall,
searching for the same hands that held and worked it so well,
swishing the fields and
felling the grass

as if surging rivers were
coursing through
a man and woman's veins
while droplets of sweat
slipped to the parched
ground and gave slivers of
hope to ants and seeds
below.

The Open Market

Huge, sprawling open market
amid Wiesbaden's cobblestoned center
near the high church spires shooting
arrows sharply skyward
towards the high heavens,
beautiful vegetables of all
sorts & sizes shine in booth after
bright stripe-covered cloth booth
like miniature suns
and the separate fish and delicatessen
trucks are wonders of ingenuity
& cleanliness to behold,
each sleek, gorgeous and
full of product just waiting
for mouth-watering consumption
by all the bag-carrying, wagon-wheeling
folks perusing all up and down the aisles
as the sun drizzles down like
a daytime ice cream sundae delight
and the U-shaped hammocks
at a nearby restaurant beckon
sweetly with open market dreams
& peaceful drifting luscious
sleep while the fountain bubbles away
and white mounds of suds drift
up like clouds and flow over the side.

The Thermal Pool

The thermal pool bubbles quietly,
warm waters soothing, smoothing,
softly surrounding swimmers in
blankets of relaxation & rejuvenation,
the darkened, elegant Wiesbaden church towers soaring
strongly against the sky seen through
the tall glass windows around the pool,
float upside down and watch the shimmering
radio-wave reflection of sunlight on the water
play on the geodesic ceiling, like a hypnotic
message from a foreign planet far away,
feel the cool air outside the pool on the wooden
deck, lean on the railing with towel on shoulders
and watch the interwoven narrow streets below,
hear snatches of a violin and cello quartet performing
for a hotel crowd across the street, cheers erupting
after the last sound dies away, the setting sun now
glinting on the towers, the temperature dropping
a degree or two, just enough to cause shivers and
force chilly gazers back inside the magic hot-house womb of
mineral waters and brilliant bouncing dancing light.

Pizza and Pasta in the Rain

Caught in the rain in Wiesbaden
outside the modern but a bit confusing
pay as you go Vapiano Italian restaurant,
big red table umbrella dripping down
on all sides,
but we're high & dry for now,
huddled together like nesting birds,
we laugh and eat our pizza and pasta
while looking out at
children riding bikes loudly through
the puddles in a cobblestoned courtyard,
impervious to anything but
the side-splitting splash of
wet and glorious fun.

Swirling

Swirling on a round children's park merry-go-round,
with vertical poles and seats that hold passengers
in place against the pull of slipping, sliding, twirling
clockwise motion, children jumping on and off,
the world spinning around in utter exhilarating confusion
full of flashing colors, words, sounds and the rush of
wind whisking by as if in a hurry to catch a bus,
German moms & tots prowling on the fringes
watching to see how long the people on board will stay
before the inevitable slow-down and leap
back to terra firma, which never ever felt so
keen and fresh and good.

Big Chess

Watching big chess pieces on a huge board
in a lush Wiesbaden park just off Wilhelmstrasse
as dusk ever so slowly falls like trickles from a
half-turned off faucet,
light swirls around the soft clouds and
chess players of all ages ponder the next big move,
smaller chess games on tables surround
the big one, some with clocks,
some with missing seats,
some with men watching from green park benches,
cigarettes in hand and smoke wafting
away like stray thoughts,
but now the big game is over
and it's time to put the pieces back in the
locked wooden bin for safekeeping
until the sun rises on another day
and the huge kings, queens and pawns
can get back to business after
a good night's rest.

Riding on the Rhine

Riding on the Rhine,
spying out wet windows
full of drips and drops
at castle ruins and vineyards
floating by on either side,
quiet down below in the
polished wood lounge,
bartender bustling up drinks
from behind his secret perch,
scrambling up the stairs on the
soaked deck & then up another
staircase to the highest point to feel
the drizzle on your face and see
the water foaming back from
the sharp prow of the ship,
exquisite gorgeous loneliness
and one-ness with the elements
with flags flapping in the stiff breeze
above and hats held onto tight,
scanning the hills and cliffs for signs of life
and what it meant to be a prince in each
neighboring little kingdom along the Rhine,
with a family castle, river rights and lush lands,
all getting rich off the boats carrying goods
passing through, and there it is, the most
beautiful little castle of all, right in the middle of the
river, magnificently preserved in every detail,
white sides and black domed towers, plus a drawbridge,
it catches your attention and slips back downstream,
playing with your imagination, just like the Lorelei on the rocks,
who called out to the sailors and sank so many ships,
the wind plays tricks and I think I heard
the siren shout to me that day, too, on the deck
with each touch of the rain on my face and softly singing soul.

In the Open Cable Car

In the open cable car swinging gently
up above the endless vineyard rows
shooting out in all directions
like an amazing crazy quilt
just beyond the town of Rüdesheim,
after a drizzly but scenic Rhine river
boat ride from easy-going Wiesbaden
(with bright sunshine and strong
surprise winds on deck on the last
river bend around the castle-strewn
side hills, whipping coats, pants
and hats like flags in a micro-burst),
there's a soft quietude that plays like
a beautiful, lulling symphony, almost
as if the Lorelei is singing to sailors
and trying to make them crash onto hidden
Rhine rocks, but here you're hanging
in space in a tiny metal car, alone with
your thoughts, hopes and dreams,
with no windows and the sky your
only neighbor, a meditation on
everything and nothing at the same time,
the river glinting, the ships moving slowly
like sugar cubes in molasses, the whole
world one big kaleidoscope of color,
the wind picks up and rocks the car a bit
and with white-knuckle happiness
you glide the rest of the way up to
the top of the hill looming tall over
the picturesque, oompah-band sized town.

In the Monastery

In the Kloster Eberbach monastery
just outside Rüdesheim,
mystical, meditational, full of sweeping
arches and quiet gardens,
deep and dark rooms are full of old wine casks
for the vineyard that now occupies
the buildings and grounds,
a heavy weathered wooden door creaks open
and tired traveler feet tread carefully
on irregular stone floors over to a worn keg table full
of lit candles that glow nobly, as if containing wisps
of the world's deep sweet knowledge amidst
the huge surrounding cask walls,
two small windows up high allowing in
just feeble bits of light in this glorious
ancient setting, small wonder many scenes
from Sean Connery's *The Name of the Rose* movie
were shot here in all this super-shrouded atmosphere,
flames surrounded by glasses of glorious Riesling
wine are soon swirled, smelled and tasted
by all hands, each in the quiet circle looking
at the small bits of fire and candle wax dripping
slowly down onto the rugged round wooden keg top,
modern explorers joining up with ancient ones
around a fire to share a story, a spoken song of long ago
between soft sweet sips of wine.

The Red Ox Inn

The Red Ox Inn
old as the Heidelberg hills,
carved with the
initials of students
investigating the
wonders of hops,
yeast and water
as well as schnitzel
and sauerbraten
served in dashing
dark corners where
light filters in only
a bit through ancient
windows, Mark Twain
even visited once
and wrote his name
in the guest book
along with countless
other famous folks
who took shelter
in the booths
and twists and turns
and creaked the floorboards
a late-night time or two.

Floating in a Pool

Floating in a Baden-Baden pool
with my two sons
splashing,
jumping,
gliding,
meditating on the lights
and colors and sounds,
as the green valley curves
away from the eye
and the woods lull with
surrounding stateliness,
elegance and history,
is there anything more
enjoyable than the sounds
of children splashing
gleefully in water,
as if the ticks of all
the eternal clocks had stopped
and all the bombs that had
ever been dropped were reversed
and wished away and Krakatoa had
simply never erupted
because there was just
too much universe-powering, fast-expanding
fun being explored as happy young bodies
in dripping swimsuits
emerge and plunge back in
with harmless war-whoops and
shrieks until exhaustion sets in
and all that can be done is to hang
tiredly on the pool ledge looking
back at your new-found

water-logged friends
who can't stop smiling as
they tilt their drenched heads
back and look up at the
clearing, cleansing
endless afternoon sky.

Watching the Scenery

Watching the Black Forest scenery
rolling, dancing, flashing by
from the big clean window of a bus,
humming along the autobahn,
curving along back roads,
spinning huge wheels through
little towns with proud churches
and welcoming gasthouses,
each happily content to be small
and part of the swirling surrounding
wooded hills that flow like green rivers
toward the dark and light,
thinking about good beer, cuckoo clocks
and Schwarzwälder Kirschtorte,
a chocolate dessert that can bring
a strong Schwabian lumberjack
to his rugged, calloused knees.

Searching for My Grandfather

Searching for my grandfather
in every Black Forest corner,
road, church, town and trail,
trying to track and soak up the essence of
his childhood in the little farming
towns of Tiengen, Seitingen and Oberflacht
where he led a somewhat romantic,
mysterious life as an apprentice
import/export agent, a mandolinist
with a beautiful voice who sang and
played well for everyone in the local pubs,
and a risk-taking motorcycle rider who ran
black market eggs, milk and supplies
over the borders during World War I,
he had curly hair, an infectious grin and
a great sense of humor and as far
as numbers went, he was astounding,
able to add up long columns of figures
in his head without a pencil or mistake,
a true entrepreneur who tried his hand
at any number of trades and businesses
in Germany and America before latching
onto a bankrupt bakery and turning it
into a successful cookie-making factory
of wonder, with all the brick-lined ovens
and conveyor lines, beautiful baking smells,
huge rolling batches of dough, an old
1920s safe with a spin dial and marvelous,
ancient wooden chairs that spun
and creaked on clever springs,
he was always on the floor under a machine

with a wrench with his brother-in-law, Reinhold,
often wearing a grease-stained apron,
and how I loved those two inventors
making things work and wheel and spin
out of thin air, as though they controlled
the entire universe with their thick calloused hands,
he lost his hearing as a young man
in Chicago due to a burst appendix infection
that spread and a bad ear operation,
so it was always a little difficult to converse,
although he read lips and had the most
powerful hearing aid available in his shirt pocket,
with wires that led up to little light beige
earbuds in his ears, sometimes it would squawk
and squeak and we'd have to tap him
on the shoulder to let him know &
he'd usually laugh and twist
a few dials on his device to tone things down,
he grew up in the same little towns
as my grandmother and great uncle
and they went to school together,
but his past is somewhat shrouded and hard to gauge
since he lived with his grandfather
after his father died in a factory
accident when he was young,
who was he and how did he come to be who he was,
how did a brilliant businessman emerge from
the motorcycle-riding young man risking it all to
bring food to those in need across the border,
where did he learn to play mandolin and
sing and how did he and my grandmother
fall in love, these things that no one knows

but the Black Forest, which only gives me glimpses
and glimmers inside between the trees,
although I can also touch the road that leads to
where he was born and where my ancestors came
from and feel the warmth of love, blood, beer,
sweat, dust and song beneath my searching, yearning hand.

Deer Bridges

Deer bridges span smoothly across the Black Forest autobahn
as sleek cars and buses speed along,
astounding curved structures filled with trees,
bushes and plants as if the forested land on one side
had thrown a tentacle across the road to the other edge
so that rabbits, deer and other animals can pass over
without a scratch,
how much planning must have gone into such
a wondrous, outlandish and expensive thing,
a curved botanic garden above the concrete,
steel and signs of man-made roads
full of vehicles that never once gave
nature a thought on the way to important destinations
in every compass direction,
but here someone took a breath and
paused to look and think
what animals might need and want
and then put such magnificent foolish ideas into motion
amidst the constant curling chaos of
blurring, whizzing, whirring wheels.

The Man in the Cage

My great-uncle Reine was
always the man in the cage,
down in the deepest darkest
basement of the bakery
where the old bits and pieces
of machinery lay,
working away in his tool room
surrounded by solid wire mesh walls
on some repair at his wonderfully
cluttered tool-bench
under a stark hanging light, as though
a man on stage about to begin
a play, every tool an artistic
brush with which he could create
the most amazing things--cut and thread
pipes, saw & glue wood, vice, bracket, nail, screw
and craft--all of the world's mechanisms and twists
and turns were his to command, and he had what seemed
like X-ray vision to look into walls and
know where plumbing, electrical and sewer
lines ran, plus a photographic memory
that could be astonishing at times,
I remember helping him install space heaters,
patch brick walls, bolt supporting wood pieces
under porches, paint steps (oh, what a beautiful,
economical brushstroke he had without making
a stray drip anywhere!), drill holes in cement to drain
away puddles (while dipping the super-hot drill bit
in a pan of water to cool it off from time to time),
climb up on roofs to clear gutters (even at age 85!)
and hop into old cast-iron basement sinks

to get at and change rusted-out pipes on the ceiling
with a huge wrench that he twirled and used with ease like
Thor's mighty mythological hammer,
he worked the family farm back in the Black Forest as a boy,
often riding a bike several miles to the village with
a large heavy metal container of milk (obtained from
cooperative cows that he milked in the barn early
each morning) strapped to his strong back,
working from sun-up to sundown without a complaint,
and he laughed as he told the story about how his older
brothers and sisters would wash his feet
at a certain time of year before carrying him over
to a wooden barrel full of water and cabbage
so that he could stomp and splash and churn the mixture
into sauerkraut, and when he wasn't tending to the farm,
he worked in the tile-factory next to their house,
digging out clay and shaping it into roofing tiles
that would be fired in the kiln,
a lover of history, and a fount of old German songs
and sayings, he was also a dapper dresser
(with the two suits he owned) who loved to eat a
good steak on occasion and may possibly have been
the kindest man the world has ever turned out,
a marvelous "third grandfather" to me (whom I called "Geity,")
who would bring the most wondrous wind-up toys
with whirring wheels and gears at Christmas,
along with delicious donuts at other times he was
doing odd jobs around our house, and I remember
driving downtown once to an early morning fruit market
with my great-uncle and grandfather in my grandfather's
burgundy Cadillac that always featured a full tank of gas,
a sparkling clean look and comfortable leather seats,

to purchase a number of huge, heavy cases of apples
in thick cardboard boxes, which would be stacked on
the enclosed porch stairs back at their Chicago two-flat,
ready for daily eating and making into Grandma Kuhn's
amazing apple and plum cakes, and thinking that they were the
two coolest older guys on the planet, and loving them like
the sun, moon and stars for taking me along on such a
magnificently mysterious early morning ride.

The Church in Oberflacht

In the quiet, farm-surrounded village of Oberflacht,
a hidden little town in the southern reaches of
the Black Forest where life is slow and people have
time to think and see the stars at night,
there's a small white church at the top of a hill
kept as neat as a pin and polished up as if it was
brand new instead of hundreds of years old
with the most amazing paintings and designs inside,
a gorgeous choir loft and organ, gleaming wooden pews,
baroque swirls here and there and an incredible
bas-relief painting/sculpture of a man and a crucifix
that seems to grow out of the wall and hang there in space,
a head-spinning but reverential combination of several
artistic mediums that boggles the mind and makes you
take a seat to contemplate how reality has just been altered,
the light streams through the windows and dances on
the floor, playing on your consciousness and soul,
making visitors think for a quiet moment about
things that have been, are now happening or might occur
in the future, and how a church, even one in a small village
that isn't on anyone's travel agenda, can grab hold of you
in a passionate soaring embrace that takes your breath away
and sends it flying out toward the nearby hills in a soothing
celebration of life, love, worship and beauty deep in the
twisting backroads of southern Germany where beer is
slowly sipped and the simple rituals of daily life are tended
closely like the finest treasures ever made.

Grandma Kuhn's Plumcake

Grandma Kuhn made the
best plumcake in the world,
so good, so sweet, so
beautiful to behold
with all of those baked plum slices
on top in a row,
sometimes I thought
mouths were watering
even in galaxies & worlds
far away.

If only I could open the door
to her kitchen once again
and smell that sweet plum
scent and see her smiling by the
oven with a wooden spoon in
hand, I'd know that the world
was safe and made to stay,
good down to the very last
luxurious bite.

Black Forest Girl

She was a Black Forest girl,
living in a small village
and working on a farm,
she once unloaded a train car
full of wood and stacked it on
her horse-drawn cart to carry
back home to fuel the fires,
she fed the large family of eight
with her sisters and learned how
to turn meals into magic at a
cooking school taught by nuns
in a convent near the Swiss border,
she knew the chickens, cows and pigs by name
and hiked in the two low nearby mountains
(Hohenkarpfen and Lupfen) to find berries and mushrooms
when the seasons for each came around,
once when she was walking through the
mysterious and darkening woods near night,
a driverless horse-drawn carriage came
wheeling at a fast pace down the road
she was walking on and as it turned a corner,
she looked inside the windows and saw no one there,
it was like something out of an ancient folk tale
and she ran quickly home to find a safe place
and tell this frightening story, but it always
stayed with her because such things happened
in those dark woods, and later, when she was a bit older
she heard the booming sound of cannons in the far-off distance
during the First World War and sent postcards to the
boys in the village who had been drafted and sent off
to fight, but eventually she became fond of a dashing young

man on a motorcycle who lived with his grandfather and
worked for an import/export firm, who could charm the
crowds with his singing and play the mandolin,
easy with good wordplay and a joke, he made everyone smile
and he turned up for dinner at her house many times
and felt like he was already part of the family,
his heart already taken by a beautiful Black Forest girl
bustling about the kitchen and farm and preparing
the most amazingly tasty meals
with a long worn wooden spoon in her hand
like a conductor directing a symphony of succulent treats.

Two-Man Crosscut Saw

The two-man crosscut saw sliced through
the log with cool ripping efficiency but only
if you got the rhythm and angle right with your
pushing-pulling partner on the other side,
sawdust flying and sweat dripping down foreheads
and arms, you work as one as well as you can
and progress jaggedly down through the wood
until the piece finally falls off and you pause and laugh
and look into each other's eyes and high-five
since you beat the other log-cutting team
up on the widened dirt and stone path in the Black Forest woods
before you head over to the big thick log where you
can try to pound long dark nails with one stroke with the
narrow backside of an axeblade or hammer (which, as it turns
out, is pretty tough to do and not many succeed), followed
by tossing a hammer end-over-end at balloons attached to a board,
you get the hang of the toss after a few tries and explode
a few for fun and then watch your youngest son nail balloon
after balloon with amazing ease as if he's Buffalo Bill, Annie
Oakley & Calamity Jane rolled into one in a Wild West Show
Shooting Contest in a huge canvas tent somewhere out in the
Dakotas, but then it's off to a timbered house down the road with
accordion music and song, good beer and schnitzel and before you
can say *"Eins, Zwei, Drei, G'Suffa!"*, everyone is up and dancing
in the center of the room, with bright wide happy smiles
as if riding on the softest highest clouds around the world and
seeing all the tiny sights below, could there be any better moment
than this that sums up the fleeting essence of life, to laugh and love
and eat and drink with family around a carved wooden table
surrounded by thick timbers and gorgeous, rollicking, magical
musical notes that wind us all together like the sturdiest twine that
rolls back in history to the earliest fires and voices lifted loud
above the crackling, warm blaze and cave-painting party din.

Sitting at a Long Wooden Table

Sitting at a long wooden table laden with food,
drink, talk and laughter on the outdoor deck of
a local restaurant near the tiny towns of Seitingen
and Oberflacht deep in the southern Schwabian reaches
of Bavaria with stunning views of the valleys, hills and
mountains all around, elbow to elbow with Black Forest
relatives who have assembled to say hello to
their American cousins who have come to call,
bits and pieces of German and English conversation
flow back and forth over the schnitzel and
sauerbraten, wurst and beer until everything is linked
together like stiches in a magnificent tapestry that starts
back in time when there were eight children (who survived
childbirth out of fourteen) in a hard-working farming/tile-making
household in a little southern Germany town not far away from
the Swiss border before they all spread out throughout Europe and
America, held together by the bonds of blood and family, all
happy to see the descendants of their parents and grandparents
once more and to view old black and white pictures of who they
were so many years ago as children in the light of day, the
waitress bustles around and clears the dishes and brings dessert
and the stories and memories flow like a soft cooling breeze on
this warm day when the tumblers in the locks of time click into
place and vault doors to the past, present and future swing open
simultaneously and present their precious gold ingots to all who
touch them and feel their bumps, scars, beauty and exquisite
lovely strength, courage and inner boldness, that inspired a few
hardy souls to leave all behind and head into the unknown of a
new country without knowing how to speak a word of that
language, to start over and begin again without any promise of
success in any way, shape or form,

to re-create themselves a second time and become someone else, like a chef creating a new dish, or a brewmaster crafting a new type of beer and taking the first cool new sip of freedom before offering his new potion to his thirsty friends, the glasses clink one last time and handshakes and embraces are offered all around before the mountains and valleys that once were home to other generations are gazed at softly once more from a red-painted deck that doubles as a magical folk tale loom and mystical mapping time machine.

Lederhosen

Lederhosen
are so crazy-looking
they make you laugh,
but then you look closely
and you can tell they're
beautifully made and
full of ornate, colorful stitching,
almost as if out of an
ancient folk tale from the Bavarian
mountains of southern
Germany, where huge alphorns
are blown, sheep are shorn
and beer is poured from carved spigots
tapped firmly with a heavy mallet into
round wooden beer kegs hoisted
up on tables by thirsty, calloused
hands used to years of rough, hard work.

The Graf Zeppelin Floats By

The huge Graf Zeppelin went
on a world tour in 1929 and
ended up in Chicago, where it
wowed the crowds below in
parks, streets and backyards,
so big it dwarfed planes flying by,
it was a real event in those days,
a beacon for burgeoning
transcontinental travel,
and some of the tall buildings even
had dirigible docking ports built in at the
top peaks, to allow people to land in style,
if you can imagine it, the Graf Zeppelin even
floated by the hospital room in Chicago where my
mother was born in mid-August of that year,
the proud parents of a newborn baby girl looked up
and saw the massive rigid airship floating by, as if signaling
the wave of the future in the world of flight
and the advent of a new luxurious way to roam the globe,
my curled-haired handsome grandfather must have
looked out the window in astonishment,
wondering how a baby could be born on the same day
that the Graf Zeppelin decided to drift slowly by,
and deep in the Black Forest, as the bus goes
rolling slowly through the city of Friedrichshaven,
there's a statue of Count Ferdinand von Zeppelin
(shown with a big bushy mustache, an airship captain's
cap and coat, and a pair of binoculars hanging down
from a strap around his neck) the conceiver of the amazing
big floating device that caught the eye and imagination
of so many people around the world, including a little
family huddled around a newly arrived baby girl named Helen,
swaddled in a soft cloth and held tight in strong arms
like the biggest sparkling star in the sky.

Carriage Ride of Dreams

The horse-drawn carriage clip-clopped
up the curving cobblestoned road at
an easy pace, heading leisurely towards
a dazzling dream castle at the top of the hill,
the stores on the sides of the street slipping by
slowly, letting you glimpse through the glass
at the goods displayed artfully inside for a
few seconds before drifting into the past,
the creaks and squeaks of the wheels and
the leather harnesses on top of the sturdy steeds
adding to the joy of the morning ride,
the sun just starting to filter in over the houses
and trees to decorate the street,
life waking up and stretching sleepy limbs once more,
your family all around you, your wife & two young sons
wide-eyed and looking all around,
absorbing the sights, sounds and culture like
a tasty surprise dish of chocolate ice cream,
at the end, the wagon circles and we get off,
ready to enter King Ludwig's fairy-tale cake topper
creation called Neuschwanstein,
full of fanciful towers, white stone walls, genuine and
completely counterfeit staircases and astonishing
craftsmanship-filled rooms dedicated to
his inner creative and arts & music-loving mind,
and best of all, on the way down the hill,
there's more ice cream and a huge
Bavarian pretzel that could feed five
hungry wood carvers who've just wandered
out of the deep dark forest all at one time,
with some scraps left over on the ground
for a few brave squirrels and birds.

Mad Ludwig's Lair

Mad Ludwig wasn't really so mad
he was just lost in his love
of fairy tales and Wagnerian operas
and wanted to create a personal
Disneyland before Disneyland's time,
with beautiful castle after castle
filled with gorgeous dreamlike
details, dining tables that rose
majestically through the floor,
rooms with waterfalls and mystic
tableaus, ornate wood carvings and elaborate
colorful fantasies, a man expressing
his creativity and artistic interests
instead of running his kingdom
like a king should,
he wanted to be a painter,
a poet, an architect,
a writer,
somebody without
a crown
to weigh him
down.

Cuckoo Clocks

So many wooden cuckoo clocks
all hanging on a wall,
clicking, ticking, tracking
the time in quiet Oberammergau,
all looking like small wooden chalets with
tiny figures cutting wood or
rotating little men and women dressed in
colorful folk outfits dancing a
continually cheerful jig,
oblivious to the fast pace of life
around them and the glorious amounts
of euros exchanging hands daily for
beautifully boxed items heading for homes
across the world,
consistent keepers of the sweeping seconds,
minutes and hours, with little chirping birds
ready to emerge and peep that an important
moment has been achieved,
all gears and weights and innards oiled
and primed for years of daily use,
dependable Steady Eddie friends
in an ever-changing world,
happy, delighted to see you and
content in their simple small village ways.

Leonardo's Madonna

Amazing young Leonardo,
just twenty-six and painting brilliantly,
ready to change the world with his
incredible ideas, drawings, art,
and science, created a wondrous
Madonna of the Carnation oil painting
that hangs now in the Alte Pinakothek
museum in Munich, so small and yet so
full of his enormous talent,
with the young Virgin Mary softly
posed with a naked child on her lap reaching
up for a red carnation in her hand,
the lighting of each detail so perfect, round
and utterly astounding that it knocks you
back a step or two and winds your thoughts
into big convoluted Bavarian pretzel knots,
who was this man who knew so much about
brushstrokes, light, color and depth at such
a tender age and why did he paint so few
works during his life, was it due to a perfectionistic
streak or a tendency to paint and repaint over things
time and time again in his works, carrying the paintings
with him as he traveled to and fro, working for kings
and other important rulers of the time, creating
plays, celestial shows, eye-opening weapons
and spectacular huge horse-statues,
perhaps there just wasn't much time to paint
after his multi-directional talents soared,
no time to sit and think and break out the easel, brushes,
and oils, too much in demand to do what he wanted to do,
a juggler of God-given gifts, torn between devoting too
much attention to one only to neglect the other,

studying life in all its spiraling nuances
and seeing it all in a beauteous Madonna and child,
her dress sleeves a luminous red that glows with the
inner pulse of life's energy itself.

The Munich McDonald's

The Munich McDonald's is mobbed,
full of eager hungry lunchtime souls lined up for
fast burgers, fries and shakes,
content to move inch by inch
toward the ordering goal while pondering
the lengthy letters of the German language menu overhead,
the sun's out, the huge fountain outside is pouring
its clear multiple H2O arches in
endless entertaining, lulling, hypnotizing half circles
that reflect the light like a thousand kaleidoscopes,
putting people in a plush painting of a Bayern afternoon
in a big, bustling city with everyone a moving or
temporarily stationary dot in a pointillistic canvas,
incomplete and ever-changing while
pedestrians, skateboards, camera-clicking tourists,
children and leaning lovers all add sound, soul
and personality to the colorful Karlsplatz collage
of life spilling out over the crowded square like
water from Ponce de León's elusive, mysterious,
unobtainable fountain of never-ending youth.

Twisting Turning Time

Clanging, clinging clocks,
twists and turns and knocks,
magical old metallic music
plays loudly across the
crowded courtyard in Munich
as the famed Rathaus-Glockenspiel's
16th century wedding scene
goes through its entertaining paces,
the jousting knights on horseback
cleverly miss each other the first two
go-rounds before the third time's the charm
and the French horseman falls back
suddenly on his steed, defeated once more
in battle by the ever-victorious Bavarian knight,
then the coopers below spin and
jig to give hope, courage and vitality
to the fearful Munich citizens of the horrid,
humbling 1517 plague year again,
before a little golden bird pops out like sunshine
from a high perch to chirp boldly at the end,
the whole show a tribute to ingenious wheel & gear
creativity and metal craftsmanship of an Alp-high
old order that touches both children
and adults in a way that only a
splendid splurge of art, imagination
and historical spectacle can,
up high and playing like a
short, joyful Broadway musical show
that's memorable, fun and
full of twisting turning ancient time.

Big Beer

Big beer on the table in
Munich's old Zum Franziskaner beer hall,
huge handle on the side,
Löwenbräu's blue lion winking back,
caught on glass,
with inverted circles in all-around surround,
caging, cajoling, controlling him,
a liter of mixed-up hops, barley, water and
secret brewing techniques
so good with schnitzel, sauerbraten,
or bratwurst with
roasted potatoes & red cabbage
on the side,
and dirndled waitresses with
black money pouches bustling
back and forth
as if in charge of all the world's gold,
liquid gold,
in huge glass mugs,
guarded by a fierce blue lion
just waiting for a chance to break
free, leap out and pounce.

The Lady from Dubai

Flying along in a cab
to the countryside outside Munich,
streets shooting by, gasthouses a blur,
restaurants registering for just a blink
and then receding like runners into the past
until the city suddenly ends and farm fields
and big green spaces take over, leaving
the crowded bricks and mortar of the
bustling metropolis full of beer, bratwurst
and business behind in the rear-view mirror
because a previously unplanned instant
"guerrilla" round of golf at a foreign location beckons,
(one completely unknown except for a name & scribbled-down
address that the somewhat confused cab driver doesn't seem
to be able to find, creeping along a dusty road full of trees,
swooping side ditches, big beautiful yellow sunflowers
and small set-back red brick houses, finally depositing
his baffled, bespectacled passenger
at the wrong place and roaring
away in a big-bang brown billowing cloud
that cloaks all objects in its tsunami-like path),
walking back down the road while huge
pieces of farm machinery ramble by and kick up more dust,
trampling through tall, foot-grabbing grasses
by the graveled sloped side to scramble out of the way,
smelling the earth and feeling lost and
lonely but on a secret mission to track down a place
that seems to have vanished into thin air,
the day thickens and bees tiredly buzz
and after another super-slow-motion half hour
of faltering footsteps, the course is finally found
and the now-weary traveler is paired up with

a ragtag rental bag of clubs and
a blonde, poised, athletic and friendly lady from Ireland
who, as it turns out, has spent the past decade in Dubai
with her robotics-expert husband before a recent move
back to Hofbräuhaus-land and she has plenty of
fantastic stories about golf and life in that sizzling,
sand-strewn mecca to tell as the ball is struck and found
and struck again, over and over,
as if on a wheel, turning constantly,
but full of ever-changing nuances
like colorful bedsheets flapping and twisting in
a light summer wind in a backyard seen from
a distance while driving by on the way to somewhere else,
the course is practically empty and well-groomed
with tall trees everywhere and the rented clubs
feel good, the elusive rhythm found on more holes than not,
walking in the sunshine, talking about travel, golf, sports
and the somewhat hard-to-fit-in Munich social life scene
until the last green is reached and the round succumbs
to totals on a scorecard, but the vitality between the numbers
vibrates electromagnetically, sending speed-of-light impulses out
into the universe to the great golf gods in the sky who watch over
the trudging, swinging, tiny people below and secretly
nod, sigh, laugh and smile.

Schneeball

Take a look at sweet "schneeball" treats
in cobblestoned Rothenburg ob der Tauber,
all sitting neatly in rows behind the glass
in the tiny bakery shop,
some colored pink, some white, some
just in mouth-watering chocolate suits,
looking like oversized baseballs of fun,
full of crunchy nuts and neat tastes,
it can't be pulled apart by hand and
must be eaten bit by bit, using the bag
it comes in to catch the crumbs that
inevitably fall like rain, the un-caught
scraps leaving a trail behind for other
dessert detectives to follow up
winding streets and past astonishingly
preserved medieval houses, storefronts
and walls, as if you were holding
an ancient time-traveling crystal snowball
in your sweet-tasting hand.

The Hotel Eisenhut

The Hotel Eisenhut
has an iron helmet for a sign
hanging right over the entrance door,
with a cool, curved wrought iron
bracket holding it up in the air,
as if this heavy metal hat appeared
out of nowhere, shot through a time-travel
cannon to the present,
it looks out of place
and yet perfectly perfect where it is
up above and seemingly ready to fall on
unsuspecting guests and visitors to
Rothenburg ob der Tauber,
a most-magnificently and mysteriously
preserved medieval town where
time stands still and sleeps so well,
inside the ancient hotel,
the staircase creaks so beautifully
it sounds like a gorgeous wooden symphony
with high and low notes & every tone
in between, can a staircase actually sound
like a musical chord, if so, this one does
and it stirs your soul and makes you think
about the thousands of people who've
walked those stairs and the carpenters
who labored amidst sawdust, hammers and nails
building it so many moons ago.

Lookin' Out

Lookin' out from a balcony in Rothenburg
towards the hills and clouds
undulating smoothly in the distance while the
spectacular sunset slinks, shimmies and shines its
soothing rays over the ancient stone fortification walls,
highlighting bits and pieces of the brick and wood,
emblazoning the tiny arrow slits with blasts of evening
beams just before night softly cloaks and falls,
as if saying goodbye to a loved one for now
until the coming, strumming next day.

Night Knows

Night knows
when to fall
and fly about
on bold,
beautiful
black wings,
soaring through streets
and diving deep
into the darkest
corners of castles,
villages and towns,
wrapping everything
in its smooth, silky embrace
like a roll of Cimmerian expanding cloth
that covers the land
and won't let it go
until the faint embers
of dawn flicker, unfurl
and spark to
start another
big, bright Ferris Wheel
turn of day.

Wet Wedding in a Weimar Park Pond

Strange wet wedding in a Weimar park pond
with friends, family and curious gawkers
all around, the bride dressed in a simple
flowing white sundress with a halo of
white flowers in her hair, the groom
decked out in a white suit with a tie,
both standing in the thigh-deep pond water
with the Maharishi-like priest preacher pastor
guru, who was also dressed in white
and throwing red and white rose petals
over the couple like gentle wedding rice,
people oohing and aahing and clicking
away with cameras of all shapes and sizes,
even a videotaping man standing in the same pond
recording this unusual but peaceful scene,
the pond crowd starts to disperse
and some find their feet sinking down into the deep
wet grass that acts like a quirky quicksand
just a few inches deep, before freeing themselves once
more to shake off the mud and sigh,
suddenly realizing as they talk with others
by the nearby stone bridge that the whole
thing is make-believe, a quaint celebration
of the earth and eco-related things,
a soft circus of something like love,
but not the real thing at all.

Ice Cream on a Bench

Eating ice cream on a bench,
eight people, six cones, two cups,
from a corner shop in Weimar
near the theater where Goethe
and Schiller put on plays
and pose now in stately statues
while the world passes by and
tree branches wave gently overhead,
a little boy whizzes past on a huge red
tricycle and zigzags around people
as if they were orange safety cones
on a fast Mercedes-Benz car-test course,
a young man strums guitar for his girlfriend
and sings a Dylan-like song,
the shops are inching toward closing time
on a sleepy Sunday and the
eight are just barely catching
the ice cream drips with their tongues before
they hit the beautiful blue-grey
cobblestones full
of sparkling bits,
a colorful cosmos
canvas beneath sixteen
happy,
resting,
tapping feet.

The Amazing Collections of August the Strong

August the Strong collected so many
amazing things while ruling the German
nation (and Poland, where he was also king)
that he must have run out of room for them all,
porcelain by the boatload, ornate gold creations,
intricate clocks, jewels, miniature cities and more,
and yet he still had time (according to local legend)
to father three-hundred and sixty-five children,
so that just about everyone in Dresden is
related to royalty, or so the story goes,
but in the Green Vault museum in mightily rebuilt
and yet still continually reconstructing Dresden,
so full of blackened sandstone that both attracts
with its brawny muscularity and repels with the
dark discoloration that covers so many buildings in
a coal ash-like hue, a number of August the Strong's
wondrous possessions are displayed in beautiful
glass cases under dim light,
some commissioned by the ruler himself, including many
by an astonishing goldsmith named Dinglinger
who could seemingly shape anything out of precious metals
down to the most microscopic, tiny detail,
for instance the huge multi-layered coffee cup
and potholder made of twenty-four carat gold
with little people sitting around a table eating &
drinking hidden inside, all just barely visible to those
who duck down a bit and peer sideways
and marvel at the royal renaissance-man king's whims,
which had so many scampering to create, collect,
shape, please and surprise.

Singers in the Square

Two older men singing
in a main Dresden square
dressed in blue military outfits
& sharp captain's caps
from the communist era days
but vocalizing now for euros per song,
sounding big, bold and agelessly good,
filling the square with fantastic fervor &
vivacious verve and meaning every single
note and word as if lamenting a strange and
puzzling time that has come and gone like a
sudden sizzling summer storm.

Salt from the Sahara

Salt from the Sahara
in an elegant small clear glass vial
on a table in a smooth, swanky
restaurant where the napkins are
white, thick and fancy
and everything and everyone is
dressed up to the nines
blows in thoughts of that
wind-strewn, swirling place
where Rommel ruled for a
few short moments with
his potent Panzer tank forces
and camel drivers & ever moving
Bedouin tribes have thrived for
thousands of years despite the
harsh daily grinding feel of
flying sand particles against eyes,
ears and flesh and the fear of the evil,
ever-shifting, mysterious sands
that can bury a man, tent or vehicle overnight
just like in the crackling-good old black and
white movie, *Sahara*, where weary, grizzled
Humphrey Bogart leads a cast of World War II
soldiers from a far-flung smorgasbord of countries
across the big desert on a beat-up old tank
to try and hold off the overwhelming
German forces for a few crucial hours;
Salt from the Sahara,
so white, so crystal-like in a timeless tube
tilted this way and that
while careful chefs labor quietly
in the distant kitchen over a leisurely

Dresden hotel dinner and children's heads begin
to topple with tiredness and the dark black pepper
in a nearby, equally exotic-looking vial turns
out to be from magical, far-off Madagascar,
an island full of cawing, cackling, wondrous
wildlife seen nowhere else on this
great big brawling glorious earth.

Little Smoker Men

Little smoker men
in all the store windows,
wooden, tiny, curved, carved,
and looking cool as lumberjacks,
chimney sweeps, old men, musicians and
beer-stein holding innkeepers, all completely
captivating and attractive and full of artistic
skill and keen-eyed amusement
—and expensive too—
but we're on a hunt through Germany
for the less costly ones my youngest son wants
to add to his little collection,
put a little tent-shaped clay item inside
and light it outside the house with a match
or lighter and put the top back on and see
the puffs of smoke come out the round mouth holes
as if the men have come alive to say hello and
tell you fun is on the way but watch out,
the top piece gets mighty hot when
the smoking is in motion, so your fingers
may do a painful polka dance if you grab
things too soon,
light up clay pieces in four or five smoker
men at a time and the smoke puff chuff
symphony begins and the smiles on
young and old faces start to grow
like tall sunflowers in
the soft summer sunshine.

Tables and Spies

The big round table sits
quietly like a wheel waiting
to turn in the beautifully
wood-paneled conference room
at Cecilienhof Palace in the
royal city of Potsdam,
where the last German crown
couple lived until 1945,
the large red tablecloth
and red high-backed chairs
complete the scene and
three small flags deck the
center of this all-important
meeting point of three world
leaders trying to hash out the
the new border lines and
what-to-dos after the German
surrender, the cigarette smoke
must have been thick as thieves,
with assistants bustling here and
there with communiques, advice
and whispered-in-the-ear asides,
a powerhouse affair with bristling
electric energy and tense negotiations
that lasted seventeen days
and turned the world in a new direction,
and just a short distance away,
the steel-girders of the Glienicke Bridge
stand ever alert and full of knowledge,
as if waiting to tell their secret stories for
visitors who tip their caps the right way

about the many clandestine Cold War spy swaps that took place there, an ever-delicate crisscross of prisoners set free to go back to their original sides, one palm-sweating slow echoing step at a time.

At the Berlin Zoo

Big old zoo
full of soft sweet dreams,
made of out-of-style cages
and dusty animal environments
& meandering paths that
seem to go on in the most
beautifully endless circles
while otters swim and dive and dunk,
you sit for a half hour or so on a bench
in front of the indoor orangutan display
and watch the dark & light orange apes run,
jump and play in peaceful bliss,
happy in a family-all-in-one place way
so pristine and unbothered
it makes it hard to tell which animals are
the ones behind the glass
and who's really there for viewing
in the tasty Wiener schnitzel and
big cup of fresh salty fries serving zoo.

Pizza in the Hotel Lobby

Hungry little traveler eyes
spy pizza on the Berlin hotel lobby menu
and grab onto it like
long-lost life preservers thrown
from heaven,
a bit of home amidst the
schnitzel blitz,
a cherished known quantity
that hits the spot and disappears
in a minute when it appears
lighting fast & piping hot,
followed by endless glasses of
beautiful chocolate milk,
cold,
cool,
fresh,
alive,
pure
gold for the soul.

The View from the Tower

Top of the metallic four-story
viewing tower
looking out over
a remaining section of the
Berlin Wall
with all its No Man's Land
fill of razor-sharp barbed wire
twists & turns, glaring trenches,
hidden mines, and low cement barriers galore
(an impossible gulf separating
families, lovers, and friends who
could only stare at each other across
the wasteland of wasted space
or just hear each other's distant
Lilliputian voices on clear quiet nights
until the next big bark blast from ever-present
guard dogs), so blisteringly stark and bleak
it almost becomes a startling, strangling
work of dense, deep cement art,
a heavy, moving tribute to a strange divided time
when bricks and mortar and wire kept
so many people apart & disconnected from the
ones they loved while the rest of the world watched
and let oppression sing its dim dark endless song.

At the Salvador Dalí Museum

At the Salvador Dalí Museum in Berlin,
there he is with the big curled mustache
and crazy wide eyes in all those photographs,
often in a sharp, flamboyant suit with a fancy cane
and beautiful women on either side,
almost like a dapper ringmaster inside
the vast and colorful circus of his own mind,
but he was also a terrific artist despite
the overblown showmanship who could
sketch and draw and paint and create like
nobody's business, as evidenced by the amazing
artwork on the walls on floor after floor,
and the mysteriously alive movies he also crafted
(which continually play on digital screens in small alcoves,
including the wondrous dream sequence from
Alfred Hitchcock's *Spellbound* flick), as well as books, sculptures,
tarot cards, even medallions
for the 1984 Los Angeles Olympic Games
an amazing amalgam of artistic output, much
of it on a smaller scale here, but his watercolors jump
out as if shot from a cannon and secret
religious fervor vibrates and intertwines with
the love of wine, women and song that pours
out on the many creativities and canvases of his
long, laughing, luxuriously enigmatic and talented life.

Red and Green Men

Red and Green Men,
on the pedestrian street-crossing lights,
telling us when to walk and when
to stop,
angular old-fashioned porkpie hats
and sharp suits,
they strut their stuff,
do their thing,
take care of business,
knock down the goods,
rockin' it like the tiny jazz hipsters they
indelibly are in eye-catching vibrant two-
dimensionality set on the edge of ultracool,
stratospherically transcending the typical dull-witted crossing
lights in other countries burdened with simple mindless colors,
instead, here are men with a purpose
(and a little humor, like guys on the inside of a good
clean Dagwood Bumstead watercooler joke) who catch
the attention of tired travelers,
end-of-day workers and eager-eyed children,
to whom the red and green men
seem almost alive,
part of an animated movie or cartoon where reality
is often bent and curved like Einstein-esque light and
turned into a world all its own,
the men say go, the men say stop,
you can't help but smile and wink back
and if you're a child, you feel as though you're winning
the war against rules and regs and school, with these
buddies of cartoon fun, tireless and true and full of
seeming subterfuge, magnificent, elegant,
ready to rumble red and green men.

The Streets of Berlin

Wandering the streets of Berlin
looking at each cement square connecting
the other cement squares covering
the earth beneath, forming a
grinning gray carpet to walk on.
the little green and red men symbols in the traffic
lights the only things
controlling my pace on this hot afternoon
with some euros in my pockets
and some strudel on my mind.

East and West

I remember crossing
through Checkpoint
Charlie in Berlin
as a young teenager
and how long the delays were
too while passports
were checked and wheeled
mirrors were rolled under
cars and buses to see if
people were bringing in
contraband or black market
goods to East Germany
or (on the way out)
smuggling daring escapees
to the west
in hidden car compartments,
it was out of a movie
something mysterious
spooky, grim and
astonishing and you
felt the deep oppression
of East Germany
when you made it through
the inspection gauntlet line,
gray, drab buildings everywhere
and sad ghostly faces on every corner,
haunted by a wall that
had broken spirits, divided families
and handed out heavy loads of loss,
and left people
falling,
reeling,
hopeless,
lost.

Inside the Bubble

In the massive Reichstag building,
after passing stringent security
measures for days via e-mail and
now scanners, searches and
bag checks, you finally pack into
big elevators like sheep and rise
into the air to gape and gaze
at the soaring glass dome bubble ramps,
sleek metal beams and completely
surrounding glass walls,
marveling for slack-jawed moments
at the engineering leaps and feats that
swirl all around as if the future is here and now,
step by step, you ascend the
sloped, curving pathways that
seem to float in mid-air, glancing out
at burgeoning, fast-building Berlin,
construction cranes in every direction
stretching up like a hundred sleeping
storks snoozing beneath the cloudy,
billowing, storm-streaked sky.

The Red Felt Hat

The red felt hat with
a beautiful soft tall feather angled
gently in the green braided rope band
around the inner center rim sat proudly
on my eldest son's head throughout
our trip, from sun-up to
sundown, taken off only
just before bed to keep it
from being crushed while
sleep swept out the extraneous
travel dust of the days and freshened
up the synapses absorbing
the off-beat bits of culture that fire
the interests of a twelve-year-old
boy, such as an astonishing
six-foot-long edible chocolate replica of the
Titanic in a wondrous confectionery shop,
or the massive, ten-foot-high scowling
metal nutcrackers guarding the entrance
to a colorful store laden with heaps of toys of
all shapes and sizes, or two huge
hard-plastic bears on a sidewalk
(one white, one black) that were put to good
use for a quick lean-over rest break with his brother,
or the parked bratwurst delivery truck
that cried out for an arms-up, bodies
curving to the right with the colorful painted
sausages on the side of the truck panel photo op,
or the purchase of a two-foot-long,
bright yellow plastic duck with a red plastic hat
that had to be carried around on buses, trains and
planes like a lucky charm to make people smile

and realize for a moment that all the super-sized fun
in life is really stored in children's hearts and minds
and especially in the beautiful
bouncing joyful inner music made by a
rockin' red felt Alpine hat on the head of a boy
looking out at the world all around
with bright stars bopping
in his movements
and imaginary brass bands playing
him boldly all the way down the street.

A Silent Prayer

(At the Berlin Outdoor Holocaust Memorial)

Hundreds of cement blocks set out like chess pieces
in endless repetitive rows, the passageways between
beckoning children and adults to wander deep
down the ramps, until the rectangles get bigger
& bigger and eventually block out the sun
so there's just distant blue sky overhead,
trapped in a huge field of giant cement corn,
nowhere to turn, nowhere to go, just
countless paths and pillars pushing down
on mind, body and soul,
lost, turning corners, hitting wrong spots,
glimpsing colors, fabrics, shadows moving
back and forth between the rows,
children giggle in the midst of hide and seek,
but claustrophobia soon sets in and the blocks
become tombs, each a reminder of what
was stolen during the war and never given back,
life, love, slaps on the back and slow-sipped beer,
everything meaningful in life stripped back
and thrown into deep muddy holes in
a devastated, devastating terrain,
know who they are and what they felt,
imprisoned, lonely, dirty, without hope
and then walk towards the freeing light,
breathe deep, turn soft and glance back at the
far-stretching sea of thick, heavy blocks
and say a prayer for all you see.

Thinking of Home

You never want a journey to end,
with all the sights & tastes & people & sounds
so foreign and strange and lovely in
ways that touch your traveler's soul
because you've stepped outside your comfort zone
and opened your mind and heart to movement,
change, culture, art and the world,
making you a different person than the one who
started out with a suitcase of clean clothing
and then exchanged it for one full of wrinkled
socks and shirts and gifts and books for
family and friends back home, where
you suddenly yearn to go, back to the familiar
bed and yard and neighbors, as well as the
wonderfully fluffy white dog who probably won't
know who you are anymore since you've been gone
so long, but as the journey winds down you know
it's time to go, to bid farewell to the fabulous
montage of things you've seen throughout Germany
which seems to be a country with precision-like
train times but wounds that are still healing between
east and west sides, with so many churches, buildings, and
museums just being rebuilt so many years after the wall
fell and communism was pushed aside, just the fact that
so much was still in rubble in eastern Germany was astonishing,
as though the communists didn't care about putting things back
together and just kept it all gray and drab and lacking color,
the whole country feels like a gorgeous vase that fell off the mantle
and split into a thousand pieces that's just being put back together
with glue while everyone wrestles with guilt over the wars and
the innocent lives tragically taken, all the apologies and thought-
provoking public artworks are still forthcoming as new generations

re-examine other generations and try to steer the ship in a new
direction that harms no one and yet gets things done,
such a beautiful country with such big mistakes,
where half of my heritage comes from, back on the Bavarian farm
in far southern Germany, cutting the wheat with a scythe and
milking the cows and making the roof tiles in winter with clay dug
from the earth, and yearning for a start in a new country, where
I'm heading now, back to where all of me is between my
well-known four walls, thinking of where I came from and where
I'm going and wondering where the next trip will lead my
ever-wandering, wondering, whistling soul.

Scythes, Spoons and Dreams

I remember the feel of the scythe in my hands
as a boy in the Black Forest, helping my cousins
cut down a small section of a field of high grass
in order to feed the cows, the power, the motion,
the swishing sound as you moved back and forth,
finding a rhythm with footwork, hands and arms,
moving through the tall grass, amazed at how
well the sharp curved blade cut, how warm my muscles
felt and how some small beads of sweat dripped down
off my forehead into the ground from the effort,
connected for a few moments to the earth, the grass
and the sky, and when I was a teenager, I helped
my great uncle swing another scythe to cut the tall fields
of grass and wildflowers in late spring in the backyard
at our house after the flowers had all
bloomed and burst into color,
such a simple, elegant but effective tool,
and to see him use it with such economical movements
was like watching a poem walking through the soft sun,
and I remember the dreams of my great uncle, grandfather
and grandmother for a better life in a new country,
which in turn created my own possibilities of dreams,
but, most of all, I recall pounding happily on
Grandma Kuhn's well-used pots and pans on the floor
in her warm, wonderful kitchen as a child with
two big, beautifully-worn and loved dark wooden spoons.

About the Author

Joseph Kuhn Carey's poetry book, *Postcards from Poland,* was selected as the third Journal of Modern Poetry Book Award winner in 2013 and published by Chicago Poetry Press (as part of the award) in February 2014. (*Postcards From Poland* is currently available at PostcardsfromPoland.com and www.Amazon.com). *Postcards from Poland* was also selected in May 2016 as the 1st Place Poetry Category winner in the Pacific Book Awards, as well as the 1st Place "Medalist" winner in the Travel Category for the 2015 New Apple Book Awards For Excellence in Independent Publishing in February 2016. In addition, *Postcards* received a Florida Writers Association Royal Palm Literary Award in November 2015 (as the 1st Place winner in the "Travel Category"), and awards from the 2016 Beverly Hills Book Awards, 2015 Midwest Book Awards, and 2015 Royal Dragonfly Book Awards, in addition to awards from the London, Paris, Amsterdam, San Francisco, Southern California, and Great Midwest Book Festivals in 2014, 2015 and 2016. Mr. Carey's most recent collection of travel poems entitled *Black Forest Dreams, A Journey Through Germany*, was also selected as the 1st Place winner in the Travel category for the 2017 Paris Book Festival, the 2016 Amsterdam Book Festival, and the 2016 Northern California Book Festival.

Joseph Kuhn Carey is also the recipient of an American Society of Composers, Authors and Publishers (ASCAP)/Deems Taylor award for music-related writing (for articles written about jazz artist/composers Carla Bley, Charlie Haden, and Anthony Braxton) and a Grammy-voting member of The Recording Academy. He's published a chapbook of poetry (*Bulk-Rate*) and a book on jazz (*Big Noise From Notre Dame: A History of The Collegiate Jazz Festival,* University of Notre Dame Press) and has released two "Loose Caboose Band" CDs of original children's songs with his brother, Bill (*The Caboose is Loose* and *Mighty Big Broom*, the latter of which garnered two first-voting-round Grammy nominations), both of which are available on iTunes and Amazon.com. He received a

Bachelor of Arts degree in English from the University of Notre Dame, a Master of Fine Arts (in Creative Writing) degree from the University of Iowa Writers' Workshop, and a Master of Science in Mass Communication degree from Boston University. He's traveled the country interviewing bakers for Bakery Magazine and written about jazz & blues artists for Downbeat, JazzTimes, and The Boston Globe. Mr. Carey's poems have been selected in the 2013, 2014, 2016, 2018, 2019, and 2020 Highland Park Poetry "Poetry Challenge" contests, 2015 and 2016 Poets & Patrons Chicagoland Poetry contests, 2014/2015 & 2018/2019 Illinois State Poetry Society Annual Poetry contests, the Journal of Modern Poetry JOMP 15, JOMP 16, JOMP 17 and JOMP 18 Poetry contests, the Writer's Digest 7th Annual Poetry Awards Contest & 80th Annual Writing Competition, Highland Park Poetry's 2013 and 2015 "Poetry That Moves" contests and the Evanston Public Library's 2013 35th Annual Jo-Anne Hirshfield Memorial Poetry Awards. Also, his poems have appeared in the Illinois State Poetry Society's *Distilled Lives* poetry collections (Volumes 3, 4 and 5), the 2014/2015 & 2015/2016 editions of the East on Central Journal of Arts & Letters, and many poetry collections published by Highland Park Poetry. One of Mr. Carey's poems was also nominated by Highland Park Poetry for a Pushcart Prize in 2019. When not scribbling entertaining poems, stories, and songs on all available scraps of paper to read to his wife and sons over dinner, he runs a successful multi-state property management business.

To order additional copies of *Black Forest Dreams* and read more about Joseph Kuhn Carey and his poetry, please visit

www.JosephKuhnCareyCreativeWorks.com